RUNNING NAKED in the SNOW

POEMS BY

LINDA JOY WALDER

ISBN: 978-1-7346737-9-1
Library of Congress Control Number: 2021941906

Printed in the United States of America.

First printing edition 2021.

Published by Free Verse Press
Free Verse, LLC
North Charleston, South Carolina

freeversepress.com

INTRODUCTION

DEAR READERS,

I'm happy that you are holding this book, because you are now a witness to Linda's heart and talent. *Running Naked in the Snow* is a diary of intimate moments made delightful by Linda's poetic voice.

You'll encounter brief but impactful moments like nightgowns and raindrops, pulling back the curtain during grief, and thinking about abandoned flowers.

You'll also experience a wildly creative book from a writer who has confidence in what makes her unique. *Running Naked in the Snow* gives you short poems about seasons, rhythm word experiments, gentle pieces about family, and more.

Pun fully intended, it was a joy to work with Linda on this book. She believed enough in my new press company to let me handle its release. I'm thankful for the friendship, and a chance to share this work with all of you.

MARCUS AMAKER

Marcus Amaker
The first Poet Laureate of Charleston, SC

For my snow angel, Daniel Jordan Fiddle
and Ava Jayne Fiddle

In loving memory of Dan Cotto

With immense gratitude:
Marcus Amaker, Poet Laureate of Charleston, S.C.
Derek Berry, Poet and Editor

TABLE OF CONTENTS

SNOW ANGEL

How It Started

It started on a January night,
no doubt a drunken celebration
toasting a Nor'easter
What other reason could there be?

Then February delivered me an
unexpected Valentine,
I was late
Not as in late for supper—Ha Ha

Next thing I knew
I had a belly,
round as his big red ball
Insider joke

After twenty-one hours,
on the 11th day of September
I held my baby boy in my arms
There are no words!!!

Five winters came and went
and the snowplows rolled on,
"time stands still for no man"
Woman, child etc. but I don't have to tell you that, you know

Once on my birthday,
the snow fell vigorously, so
we decided to make a snowpal
Gender neutral

Suddenly I saw my son, clothes flying,
laughing exuberantly,
joyful in the moment
I did not realize until now, that was his birthday gift to me

Of all life lessons learned
None taught me more, than
running naked in the snow
Pray

SNOW SCAPES

Running Naked in the Snow

On magical evenings
when tree branches drizzle with snow-shine,
I notice how streetlights cast serendipitous
shadows on the icy sidewalk.

After morning's awakening
I stand frozen at the open door,
where a vast wilderness of whiteness
confronts my courage.

Then wondrously,
I hear the urging of angels
to abide the decree of my destiny.

It is time now, I know,
to run naked in the snow.

Anchor

I am an anchor
sinking to the bottom of the sea
while a rainbow of fishes
swim unfazed
by my disturbing behavior.

Landing in the sandy granules
my life lies flatly,
accentuated by the eerie
silence of sublime choice.

Below boisterous waves
I lie blissfully unreported
content in my corporal commission
that one day will be
discovered, unmoored and misunderstood.

Editing

One summer at the Cape
on the beach with my brothers
we wore bright colored sweatshirts,
the wind swept through our curly hair.

We were one divided in thirds.

I loved those boys so much
it brings tears to my eyes remembering
our teasing,
silly laughter,
watching them play basketball
from my window,
their curly hair soaked with sweat.

We were three parts of the whole.

The day our parents called a meeting
to announce their divorce
I cannot remember if they cried
because my eyes were waterfalls of my own tears.

None of us would ever be the same again
but we would not speak of that day
or the other miserable ones.

We became three separate pieces,
surviving in our own ways,
in our own lives,
across state lines and untraveled bridges,
three curly haired children,
with less of that now
and less of everything really.

Requiem for Dr.Seuss in the Key of Dickinson

Around the bottom of a tree
He picked a twig on bended knee
The twig he thought possessed a flea
But that was not to be
So then he sought to drink a tea
Sweetened by honey from the bee
However he was not thirsty
And found his thoughts back on the flea
So tried again to look and see
On where that pesky flea could be
As if by will he could decree
The flea's return on bended knee
Alas the flea he could not see
Danced happily and fancy free
Upon the twig that fell from tree
Twas much much smaller than was he
The flea the man had tried to see
But who had won the victory
Was it the man or was it flea
The flea he won don't you agree
Perplexed the man on bended knee
Who scratched his head beneath the tree.

The Compromise

The day began with raindrops,
where you are.
I lounged in my nightgown
while the sun wandered through
a slit in the curtains,
where I am.

I am in no rush where I am,
listening to chirping birds
nesting in the tree near
my open window
suits my pace.

You are always in a hurry,
running errands,
making schedules,
your soaked umbrella
has been a dozen places before noon.

Do you think I am wasting my time?
Your time?
You want answers
I do not have.

Maybe tomorrow though
I will put on a flowing dress
and dance in the rain with you,
but no umbrellas
okay?
We should compromise.

If the rain stays,
if you do,
if I do.

Metamorphosis

Poetry.

Recognized, but not easily understood,
more resembling when the roof caves in
leaving fragments on the ground,
amazing,
upsetting,
now what?

Should you use the broom to sweep up little piles methodically
or bring the mighty force of the vacuum to inhale the particles?

I, for one,
stand back,
awe-struck
how architecture formed becomes
another matter.

Really, the process was happening slowly
beneath the surface pulsating,
in a purposeful progression,
evolving.

Sensory Deprivation

I saw the fine line of a soul
running down the street screaming

Did you see it too?

I heard cheers chasing after me

Did you hear them too?

I tasted sugary raindrops

Did you taste them too?

I felt a bullet ejected from someone's mouth pierce my skin

Did you feel it too?

I smelled fish that tasted like chicken

Did you smell it too?

All I am asking is for validation

Do you get it?

SNOW DRIFTS

Deputies

Since you departed,
your deputies watch me
from the house across the street.

Their grey-feathered uniforms
are not concealed
by the neighbor's silver roof
where they perch
gossiping and reporting.

I pull back the curtains
surmising you sent
this lineup of little lieutenants to look
inside.

I imagine they can hear my mind reciting
the ordinary and immortal
compositions of my consciousness.

Drab days without your deputies
fill me with dread until
I am revived by the vibrant sun
like a flashing squad car light
signaling to look.

Seeing your deputies' heads
bobbing vigorously again in conversation
instills a delightful sense of security within me
knowing you have dutifully dispatched them
to remind me
your promise of protection remains.

The Rose

With the grace of a rose
gradually opening to greet the morning sun,
she entered the room,
not aware of her beauty,
not looking for him or anyone.

He noticed her though,
eyes gazing over the edge of his glass,
sipping tastes of wine,
watching her body sway,
every space within him stimulated.

The morning after,
eyes gazing over the edge of his newspaper,
he enjoyed how her body moved
under a sheer nightgown,
the air scented by her sweet nectar.

In time, he grew to understand
her rose-like temperament,
delicately layered,
protected by copious prickles,
sharply-toothed,
designed for survival.

Years later,
when his smooth skin
became fine lines and scars,
he would have their time together,
keeping him company,
gently caressing his mind,
like the fragrance of a rose
lingering.

Summer-Camp Playlist

The Greyhound bus pulled out of the parking lot,
Mom, dad, kid brother and dog walked back to their car

One hundred bottles of beer on the wall
One hundred bottles of beer
You take one down and pass it around
Ninety-nine bottles of beer on the wall

She wiped the tears from her cheeks with a Camp tee-shirt,
Traded three Archie comic books for Bazooka

Down by the Old Mill Stream
Where I first, not second but first,
Met you, not me, but you

She felt very far away from home as the candy flowed,
The mountains became taller and greener

Miss Lucy had a steamboat
The steamboat had a bell
Miss Lucy went to heaven and
The steamboat went to hell

One more hour to go,
Then she would know her bunkmates and counselors

Boom, Boom Ain't it Great to be Crazy
Boom, Boom Ain't it Great to be Nuts Like Us
Boom, Boom Ain't it Great to be Craaaazy

She closed her eyes and dreamed about socials and color war
Capsizing the canoe on the lake would be fun

What is the meaning, meaning, meaning
Of all these flowers, flowers, flowers
It is the story, story, story
The story of love from me to you chachacha

Suddenly the Greyhound bus jerked to a stop
They had arrived

Friends, Friends, friends, we will always be
Whether in fair or in dark stormy weather
Camp Tyler Hill will keep us together

Twenty-six days until visiting day,
Her heart skipped beat as she leaped into summer camp.

Doors

One day,
take a giant step into yourself,
beyond the rolling waves of consciousness
split off from your life
into a parallel universe
where your past lives behind doors.

Doors, shut firmly protecting irreplaceable treasures,
you, sitting at the kitchen high-top eating tuna fish sandwiches
while your grandmother listened unconditionally.

Doors, never fully closed,
you, grieving after cancer stuck a knife into plans
with your soulmate who shared your life.

All the doors you have built protect your heart like a glorious shield.

One day,
view the doors as monuments of your past,
astonished in the wake of your resiliency
run your hands gently over your limbs,
truly alive, then
take a giant step forward!

Postcards

Inhaling the pink roses at Orvieto
lining the pathway to the Church,
farmers and local prophets
prayed for fertile land and families
with "All Our Good Wishes,"

Sipping Prosecco
at a café on a cobblestone street
under a blue sky
looking into his blue eyes
I had to close my own eyes to take it all in,
this can never end
with" All Our Love,"

Riding the high-speed train to Venice
where we were lost willingly
in a maze of streets
exploring shops filled with glass beads and silk linens
with "All Our Best,"

Dancing at St. Marks' square
under thousands of stars
street musicians filled the air with Bocelli
we breathed as one
with "All Our Hearts."

Abandoned Flowers, A Fairy Tale

Down the road,
in an alley,
abandoned flowers swayed longingly,
their tiny hearts reaching for
warmth from the sun.

After bees and butterflies drained them,
abandoned flower heads hung,
their emptied petals depleted, and
ashamed by the usage.

Abandoned flowers, were always terrified
when the sun was gone,
aloneness starkly exposed them in moonlight, and
their feelings of unworthiness.

One morning,
when dewy droplets hung from blades of grass,
a fluffy, white dog
resembling a snowball arrived and
excitedly sniffed the squishy soil.

The stems stood stoically
at first,
then relaxed,
realizing the curious canine
wanted only to explore.

The fluffy, white dog returned often,
sniffing, never disrupting,
until one sweltering afternoon
a peculiar, unfamiliar high-pitched noise
filled the air
followed by a mysterious sighting.

Approaching the abandoned flowers,
gleeful noise gently caressed a handful of flower necks, and
inhaled their sweet scent

savoring each morsal of fragrant air,
seemingly enriched by the aroma.

Thereafter, abandoned flowers blossomed,
exalted by their pleasurable potency,
finally feeling valued, and
they lived happily ever-after.

born a tree redux (written at age 10)

remember the tree
where you used to be

born so fresh and
born so free
born so happy
that's a tree

born with green leaves and
a smooth, white bark
born to be the home of a
squirrel in a park

born so fresh and
born so free
born so happy
that's a tree

where you used to be
remember the tree

SNOW FALL INTERLUDE

Winter

Under the moonlight
glistening snowflake crystal
shards cut crisp night air

Spring

Sun awakes soil
where buds break free from bondage
igniting rebirth

Summer

Birds chirping beats with
cicadas on tambourines
arouse steamy nights

Fall

Sapphire colored
jewels embellish foliage's
farewell to tree limbs

SNOW FLAKES

Happiness

Where does happiness reside?

We strive for it all of our days,
often not recognizing the presence of its lightness
yet surely feeling the heaviness of its departure.

Fearful we are that too much happiness will betray us,
though not enough will spay us,
how can the drops of rain needed to satiate the earth be counted?

Searching for happiness is like
looking for a perfect shell upon the beach
drawn in by the tide,
then washed away
all at once.

Chocolate and Marshmallow Memories

The moon looked like a marshmallow
someone took a giant bite from
in the dark-chocolate sky.

Staring up,
her mind drifted to campfires in Maine
when gooey s'mores dripped
marshmallow- chocolate lava on her bare knees,
how she loved the Hershey's- syrup chocolate cake
with marshmallow cream in the center
her Nana made twice a year
for St. Patrick's Day and her birthday sleepover, and
the utter delight of frozen Mallowmar
chocolate-coated marshmallow cookies
that could be relied upon to
greet her after school when no one else cared.

Breathing in the night air
she wondered if
chocolate and marshmallow memories
become stars?

About Face Proclamation

My face is going to age well!

White teeth glistening like
fresh fallen snow,
blue eyes dancing like
Caribbean waves,
nose hanging gracefully like
a half-opened umbrella,
delicate lips opening like
slivers of rose petals.

The tiny creases under my eyes, and
the circle of pencil lines around my neck
will not make me walk quickly pass mirrors,
nor will I Botox, detox or outfox
Mother Nature with cunning tricks.

My face is going to age well like
the woman it belongs to!

New Life

You can never get your old life back.
It is gone.
It is ghosts
Dancing in the darkness of your mind
Or morning light shining upon your heart.

You will get flashbacks
But your longings
Steal pointlessly from the present
Where your life is growing
and changing,
Like the garden you planted that amazes you
Or the string of stars that take your breath away.

Your life is full of awe and pain.
Open the portal.
Emerge from the depths of the ocean
To see a different land
Untraveled,
Waiting for you to put your footprints upon it.

A little scat a skanky

In a house worn and janky
lived a guy strange and skanky
drank from the toilet tanky

dowapdowapdowapdowapdo

legend said he'd turned wanky
momma cried in her hanky
'bout the guy strange and skanky

bibibidibibidipopbidbibo

he liked a little spanky
that wanky stanky Yankee
from North Jersey named Frankie

dowapdowapdowapdowapdo

no matter what y'all thanky
don't judge poor ol' Frankie
drank from the toilet tanky

bibibidibibidipopbidbibo

Moments

When baby's breath kisses daddy's cheek,
the universe of beating hearts vibrate.

When dogs devour bones on the back-porch
the pleasure of enjoyment is communicable.

When a child lays limply in his bed
the order of nature is defied.

When silence holds a hand
the call of heaven forbodes.

Meditation

Floating on breezes,
cushioned by clouds,
gliding over mountaintops,
eyes half open,
a Robin smiles at me.

He cannot believe how feathery
something so big and clumsy can be.
I laugh and go higher and higher.

Blanketed by warm sand,
granules rubbing toes,
fingering seashells,
a Seagull sniffs me.

He cannot believe how salty
the smell exuding from my mouth can be.
I breathe and go deeper and deeper.

Running on lighter fluid,
darting past strangers,
flying across streets,
a Pigeon tries to catch me.

He cannot believe how sprightly
a spirit can be.
I wave and go by and by.

SNOW STORMS

by the numbers

Jack died today
after a 10 wheel- chairs
1000 doctor appointments
with 200 medical professionals who called him special,

seventy- five home care workers stood at his grave weeping
fifty shovels of dirt covered his casket buried next to his father's
who died too young at 54,

after 40 grievers went home
his one mother
stood at the grave.

Anxiety

Anxiety is the winter wind that cuts
through your clothing,
startling your skin,
leaving you violated by the invasion.

After the sirens are distant, and
the shock has subsided,
you wrap a familiar blanket around your still shaking body
finding its comfort inconclusive.

The work of sanity is endless,
solving one problem, encountering another
but sometimes things sparkle and shine, and
you capture your care-free reflection in the mirror
as you fly by freely.

In those rare moments,
you're a newly hatched sparrow
undaunted by imaginary danger or real terror,
until reality snaps you back to
remembering past assaults, and
how brutally they broke you.

Chain of Angel Oaks
L'dor vador

Angel oaks hold history in their trunks,
stories of good and evil
endlessly threaded in layers of bark
protecting the continuum of generations.

L'dor vador nagid godlecha
(From generation to generation, we will tell of Your greatness)
L'dor vador... we protect this chain
From generation to generation
L'dor vador, these lips will praise Your name.

Tumultuous times have stirred
tree buds who carry traumas
inflicted by nature and nurture,
their afflicted roots have poison running through them.

L'dor vador nagid godlecha
(From generation to generation, we will tell of Your greatness)
L'dor vador... we protect this chain
From generation to generation
L'dor vador, these lips will praise Your name.

Battles break branches,
mangled parts reformed unimaginably,
none discarded as unworthy
all compost life's soil.

L'dor vador nagid godlecha
(From generation to generation, we will tell of Your greatness)
L'dor vador... we protect this chain
From generation to generation
L'dor vador, these lips will praise Your name.

Together,
leaves, branches, buds and moss
presently,
existing parts of an eternal process.

L'dor vador nagid godlecha
(From generation to generation, we will tell of Your greatness)
L'dor vador... we protect this chain
From generation to generation
L'dor vador, these lips will praise Your name.

Death like birth
embraced by Angel oaks
from generation to generation,
twisted by imperfection,
surviving in dimensions of beauty and ugliness.

He Slipped Away

If only he could sneeze,
with such thunderous force
all of the toxin filled cells
housed in mucous membranes and body systems
would expel with tornado velocity
the build-up of
packs of Marlboros,
gallons of Makers Mark bourbon and
greasy sausage and pepper sandwiches.

Clogging.
Suffocating.
Gone.

Light and free,
he would glide like a skater smoothly
over the crackled-glass-like shards
cutting through his body,
becoming more aligned with
his unencumbered soul.

Partaking.
Savoring.
Content.

He died in early October,
before the leaves turned,
slipping away so quickly without fanfare or farewell,
a guest who disappeared from the party
but not unnoticed.

Peacefully.
Gracefully.
It was so him.

Lesson

I can show you the sea
but I can't force you to
walk the beach collecting shells
or let ocean water swim between your toes.

I can show you the mountain
but I can't force you to
climb the slippery edges up
or prevent you from falling.

I can show you the basics
or the more complex,
but only you
decide to ignore or discover.

You decide for you,
but remember I decide for me.

No matter,
I'll blow you a kiss,
I'll say happy journey.

They Wrote How We Won!

Elitists
Won't defeat us!

The halls of justice will ring
Unheard voices will sing
"Ask not what your country can do for you; ask what you can do for your country?"
Kennedy wrote enslaved and free!

Technocrats,
Bureaucrats,
Media fat cats,
Beware!

Politicians,
You're fake magicians
"Do I contradict myself? Very well, then I contradict myself"
Whitman wrote poor and wealthy!

Hollywood perched on a hillside of greed,
Slide down and concede
"Rather than love, than money, than fame, give me truth"
Thoreau wrote old and youth!

Reddish,
Whitish,
Bluish,
America!

It's time to unite,
We no longer need to fight.
"What you do speaks so loudly, I cannot hear what you say"
Emerson wrote not to play!

We won!

Have Faith

Broken-winged bae,
somewhere deep inside
you know flight will return
on wings reopened.

Oh precious bird,
having flown through harsh rain
beating upon your fragile wings,
praise how you landed.

Little bird,
soon you will paint
a masterpiece across the sky,
all blue and pink and grey
with sparkling-gold striae.

Darling creature,
now find your nest,
you are deserving
nourishment and rest,
until you fly again.

Linda Joy Walder has written poetry in her mind daily since childhood. Now, the time has arrived for her to share her creations with a debut collection of works, deeply rooted in a lifetime of magical and mournful circumstances.

As the Founder and Director of a trailblazing not-for-profit organization, Linda has led the global community for the past 20 years in accepting, valuing and supporting the diversity of adults diagnosed with Autism. Her personal journey of resiliency and hope has inspired the Autism community and beyond who gravitate towards Linda's compassionate and innovative spirit.

Linda resides in Charleston, South Carolina along with her beloved family of human and furry beings.

www.ingramcontent.com/pod-product-compliance
Lightning Source LLC
LaVergne TN
LVHW012340100826
845148LV00018B/3216